Team Spirit

THE WASHINGTON REDSKINS

BY

MARK STEWART

Content Consultant
Jason Aikens
Collections Curator
The Professional Football Hall of Fame

NORWOOD HOUSE PRESS
CHICAGO, ILLINOIS

Meet the Redskins

Football players love to get dirty. Earth, mud, grass, blood—the more "good stuff" they get on their uniforms, the more they seem to enjoy a game. It is hard to imagine a team that gets dirtier than the Washington Redskins. They know that games are often won and lost at the **line of scrimmage**, and that is where they have always done their best work.

The people who root for the Redskins value loyalty, community, and *tradition*. Many of the young fans who go to games today had great-grandparents who cheered for the Redskins. They sing the same fight song that echoed through the stadium in the 1930s.

This book tells the story of the Redskins. Each player who wears the burgundy-and-gold Washington uniform understands that he is a link between the team's proud past and promising future. His job is to play football the Redskins way—with determination, strength, and spirit.

Chris Cooley raises an arm in triumph as he follows teammate Santana Moss into the end zone in a game against the Jacksonville Jaguars.

Way Back When

The Great Depression of the 1930s was a time of hardship for millions of Americans. For George Preston Marshall, it was a time of opportunity. He was a successful businessman who owned a chain of **laundromats** in the Washington, D.C. area. Marshall loved sports and entertainment. He believed that owning a team in the **National Football League (NFL)** would be a good way to combine these interests. He bought a team in Boston, Massachusetts in 1932 and named it the Braves. One year later, he changed the name to Redskins.

The Redskins had a good team. Their early stars included Turk Edwards, Cliff Battles, Ernie Pinckert, Jim Musick, and Wayne Millner. Yet try as he might, Marshall could not draw fans to his team's games. In 1937, he moved the Redskins' "home" to Washington. That season, they signed their first great passer, Sammy Baugh.

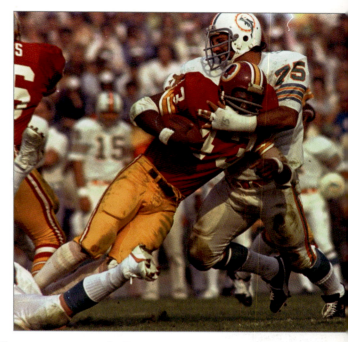

LEFT: Cliff Battles, Sammy Baugh, and Wayne Millner celebrate in the locker room after winning the 1937 NFL title.
RIGHT: Running back Larry Brown smashes into a tackler during Super Bowl VII.

Under Baugh, Washington finished atop the NFL's **East Division** in 1937 and four more times between 1940 and 1945. The Redskins were league champions in 1937 and 1942. The stars of those great teams included ends Bob Masterson and Joe Aguirre and **linemen** Dick Farman, Steve Slivinski, and Willie Wilkin.

After Baugh's playing days were over, the Redskins went into a long *slumber*. They had only a handful of winning seasons during the 1950s and 1960s. Perhaps the biggest reason for Washington's poor record was Marshall's unwillingness to sign African-American players. During those years of great racial tension, he feared that white fans in the South would not root for black players. It took a personal *plea* from President John F. Kennedy to convince Marshall that he was wrong.

After several *decades*, the Redskins rebuilt their team and were winners once again in the 1970s. They mixed young stars such as running back Larry Brown with experienced players, including

7

quarterback Billy Kilmer, safety Pat Fischer, and linebacker Chris Hanburger. The Redskins were champions of the **National Football Conference (NFC)** in 1972 and played in **Super Bowl** VII.

The Redskins continued to win in the 1980s and 1990s, after new team owner Jack Kent Cooke hired Joe Gibbs as Washington's head coach. Those teams were led by four talented quarterbacks—Joe Theismann, Jay Schroeder, Doug Williams, and Mark Rypien. Their other stars included John Riggins, Art Monk, Darrell Green, Charles Mann, and Mark Moseley.

Washington's best weapon was its offensive line. Nicknamed the "Hogs," they were the best **blockers** in the NFL for many years. The Hogs controlled the line of scrimmage and wore down opponents with their determined and *disciplined* play. The Redskins were not always an exciting team to watch, but their fans loved them because they were winners. Washington played in four Super Bowls during this period and won three of them.

LEFT: Joe Theismann, Washington's leader in the early 1980s.
ABOVE: Jack Kent Cooke, John Riggins, and Joe Gibbs share the game ball after Washington's victory in Super Bowl XVII.

The Team Today

The Redskins play in one of the league's most rugged divisions, the **NFC East**. Each season, they play at home and on the road against the Dallas Cowboys, Philadelphia Eagles, and New York Giants. Since their season almost always comes down to how they do in their battles against these great rivals, the Redskins build their teams to win these important games.

The key to winning for Washington is to find strong offensive linemen who block for powerful running backs. The Redskins also encourage their tacklers to be aggressive and hit hard. They try to wear down their opponents with smart, disciplined football. This creates opportunities for the Redskins' quarterbacks, receivers, pass rushers, and defensive backs to make game-winning plays.

Washington's victories may not be exciting compared to those of other NFL teams. But to Redskins fans there is nothing sweeter than a "boring" victory over an NFC East opponent and a run through the **playoffs** toward the Super Bowl.

Jon Jansen congratulates Antwaan Randle El after a touchdown during the 2006 season.

Home Turf

The Redskins have played in some of the most famous sports arenas in the United States, including Fenway Park in Boston and Griffith Stadium and D.C. Stadium (later renamed Robert F. Kennedy Stadium) in the nation's capital. The Redskins played there for more than 30 years.

In 1997, the team moved to a new field called Jack Kent Cooke Stadium in Landover, Maryland. Cooke had owned the team during its three Super Bowl victories. In 1999, the team's new owner, Daniel Snyder, renamed the stadium FedEx Field.

The game is only part of the experience at FedEx Field. Thousands of fans enter the stadium two hours before kickoff to enjoy the live music provided by the team. After every game—win or lose—the Redskins throw a two-hour "fifth quarter" party under the stands.

BY THE NUMBERS

- *There are 91,665 seats in the Redskins' stadium. It is the largest in the NFL.*
- *The stadium cost more than $250 million to build in 1997.*
- *As of 2007, the Redskins had retired only one jersey, Sammy Baugh's number 33.*
- *The Redskins defeated the Arizona Cardinals in **overtime**, 19–13, in their first regular season game in their current stadium.*

The crowd cheers the Redskins during a home game.

Dressed for Success

For more than 70 seasons, the Redskins uniforms have featured a combination of burgundy and gold. In their early years, the players wore gold pants and a dark jersey with the likeness of a Native American on the front. Today, the Redskins are one of the few teams that wear their white uniforms at home and dark uniforms on the road. Coach Joe Gibbs started this tradition in 1981.

The Redskins have always used burgundy and gold as their helmet colors. The team added a *logo* in the late 1950s—for several years it was a feather design, and then an arrow design. The Redskins switched to the letter R inside a circle in 1970 and began using their current logo two years later.

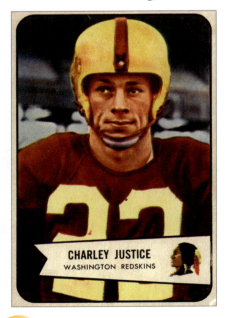

Washington is one of several **professional** sports teams with a name that many people find offensive. The word "Redskin" is considered a slur by many Americans. The Redskins believe their name symbolizes a proud tradition and do not plan to change it.

Charley Justice, in the team's gold helmet and burgundy jersey of the early 1950s.

The football uniform has three important parts—

- Helmet
- Jersey
- Pants

Helmets used to be made out of leather, and they did not have facemasks—ouch! Today, helmets are made of super-strong plastic. The uniform top, or jersey, is made of thick fabric. It fits snugly around a player so that tacklers cannot grab it and pull him down. The pants come down just over the knees.

There is a lot more to a football uniform than what you see on the outside. Air can be pumped inside the helmet to give it a snug, padded fit. The jersey covers shoulder pads, and sometimes a rib protector called a flak jacket. The pants include pads that protect the hips, thighs, *tailbone*, and knees.

Football teams have two sets of uniforms—one dark and one light. This makes it easier to tell two teams apart on the field. Almost all teams wear their dark uniforms at home and their light ones on the road.

Clinton Portis runs for daylight in the team's 2006 uniform.

We Won!

The Redskins were in their sixth NFL season—and their first in Washington—when they won the 1937 **NFL Championship**. The team was led by "Slingin'" Sammy Baugh, a **rookie** from Texas who threw the ball with tremendous speed and accuracy. Baugh played

quarterback and **tailback** and was in total command of the team's offense. He would take a handoff and either run, pass, or punt. On defense, Baugh was one of the best pass defenders in the NFL. The Redskins also had Cliff Battles in their backfield. He was the league's top runner that year.

The Redskins defeated the Chicago Bears for their first championship in an exciting game. Chicago led at halftime, but Baugh threw three touchdown passes in the third quarter to give Washington a 28–21 victory. He passed for 354 yards in the game, which broke the previous record for an NFL Championship.

Washington's next championship came in 1942. The Redskins defeated the Bears again, this time by a score of 14–6. Although the fans at Griffith Stadium were overjoyed, there was also a feeling of sadness among the players. World War II was underway. The Redskins sent a total of 44 players to battle during this period. They still had enough talent to play for the NFL title again in 1943 and 1945 but lost both times.

Washington fans had to wait 40 years before they could celebrate another championship. In 1982, Russ Grimm, Joe Jacoby, and Jeff Bostic formed the heart of an offensive line that created huge openings for running back John Riggins and gave quarterback Joe Theismann all the time he needed to pass. The Redskins powered their way to Super Bowl XVII and defeated the Miami Dolphins.

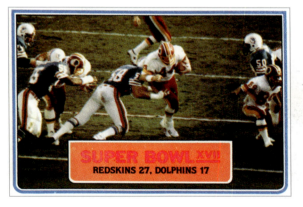

Washington trailed in that game 17–13 in the fourth quarter and faced a fourth down on Miami's 43 yard line. Coach Joe Gibbs decided to try for a first down. Riggins took a handoff, cut around the left side of the line, ran over a tackler, and sprinted into the end zone for the winning touchdown.

LEFT: Sammy Baugh looks for an open receiver during the 1942 NFL Championship game.   **ABOVE**: This trading card shows John Riggins powering through the Dolphins in Super Bowl XVII.

Five years later, the Redskins faced the Denver Broncos in Super Bowl XXII. The fans expected a great day from Denver quarterback John Elway. Instead, they saw Washington's Doug Williams throw four touchdown passes in the second quarter on the way to a 42–10 victory.

Williams had started the season as the backup to Jay Schroeder. Another Washington substitute, running back Timmy Smith, ran for 204 yards and two touchdowns.

The Redskins won their fifth championship against the Buffalo Bills in Super Bowl XXVI by a score of 37–24. Washington confused Buffalo with a **no-huddle offense** and flooded the field with four and five receivers on many plays. In a duel of strong-armed quarterbacks, Mark Rypien of the Redskins outplayed Jim Kelly of the Bills. The Washington defense also had a marvelous game. They **intercepted** four of Kelly's passes and held star running back Thurman Thomas to just 13 yards.

ABOVE: Doug Williams is jubilant after defeating the Broncos in Super Bowl XXII. **RIGHT:** Mark Rypien, one of Washington's heroes in Super Bowl XXVI.

Go-To Guys

To be a true star in the NFL, you need more than fast feet and a big body. You have to be a "go-to guy"—someone the coach wants on the field at the end of a big game. Redskins fans have had a lot to cheer about over the years, including these great stars …

THE PIONEERS

CLIFF BATTLES   Running Back

- BORN: 5/1/1910   • DIED: 4/28/1981
- PLAYED FOR TEAM: 1932 TO 1937

Cliff Battles was the first player to run for 200 yards in a game, and he led the NFL in rushing twice. Battles quit the NFL after an argument over his 1938 salary, leaving fans to wonder what might have been.

SAMMY BAUGH   Quarterback/Running Back/Punter

- BORN: 3/17/1914   • PLAYED FOR TEAM: 1937 TO 1952

Sammy Baugh could do it all. In 1943, he led the NFL in passing, punting, and interceptions. During one game that season, he threw for four touchdowns and intercepted four passes. In 1947, Baugh became the first player to pass for more than 2,500 yards in a season.

BOBBY MITCHELL   Receiver

• Born: 6/6/1935   • Played for Team: 1962 to 1968

Lightning speed, quick moves, and excellent balance made Bobby Mitchell one of history's hardest players to tackle. He led the NFL in catches once and receiving yards twice. Mitchell was the Redskins' first African-American star.

SONNY JURGENSEN   Quarterback

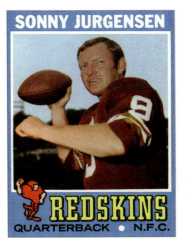

• Born: 8/23/1934
• Played for Team: 1964 to 1974

Sonny Jurgensen had a strong arm and an iron will. He waited until the last moment to throw his passes, knowing he was likely to be hit hard. Jurgensen led the NFL in passing yards three times with the Redskins.

LARRY BROWN   Running Back

• Born: 9/19/1947
• Played for Team: 1969 to 1976

Despite being hearing impaired, Larry Brown led the NFC in rushing twice and was the NFL's **Most Valuable Player (MVP)** in 1972. A special hearing aid was installed in his helmet so he could hear plays in the huddle and signals on the field.

LEFT: Cliff Battles   **TOP RIGHT**: Sonny Jurgensen
BOTTOM RIGHT: Larry Brown

MODERN STARS

JOE THEISMANN   Quarterback

- BORN: 9/9/1949
- PLAYED FOR TEAM: 1974 TO 1985

Joe Theismann was a quick and clever quarterback who led the Redskins to victory in Super Bowl XVII. He was named the NFL's Most Valuable Player in 1983.

JOHN RIGGINS   Running Back

- BORN: 8/4/1949
- PLAYED FOR TEAM: 1976 TO 1979 & 1981 TO 1985

When John Riggins got his muscular 230-pound body in motion, he was

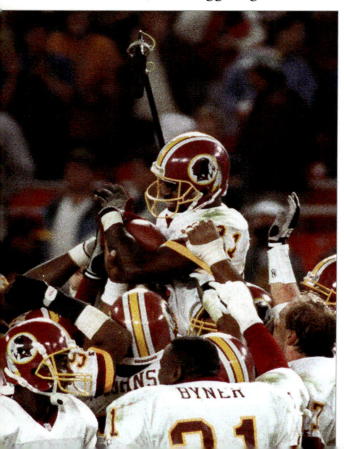

very difficult to tackle. The Redskins gave him the ball when they needed tough yards, and Riggins rarely disappointed them. In 1983, he set an NFL record with 24 touchdowns.

ART MONK   Receiver

- BORN: 12/5/1957
- PLAYED FOR TEAM: 1980 TO 1993

At 6' 3", Art Monk was one of the NFL's tallest receivers during the 1980s. He liked to catch short passes and then dodge his way down the field. In 1992, he set an NFL record for most receptions in a career.

LEFT: Art Monk celebrates his NFL receiving record.
TOP RIGHT: Darrell Green
BOTTOM RIGHT: Santana Moss

DARRELL GREEN — Defensive Back

- BORN: 2/15/1960
- PLAYED FOR TEAM: 1983 TO 2002

Darrell Green was the fastest man in the NFL for many years. He intercepted at least one pass in 19 of his 20 seasons in a Washington uniform.

CHAMP BAILEY — Defensive Back

- BORN: 6/22/1978
- PLAYED FOR TEAM: 1999 TO 2003

Champ Bailey started every game the Redskins played during his five years with the team. He intercepted 18 passes and was named to the **Pro Bowl** four times.

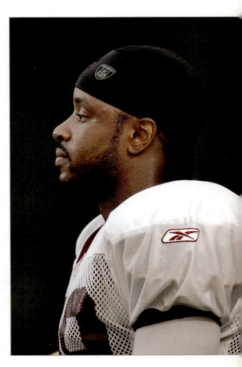

SANTANA MOSS — Receiver

- BORN: 6/1/1979
- FIRST SEASON WITH TEAM: 2005

When the Redskins decided they needed a "big play" receiver for their offense, they traded for Santana Moss. He caught 84 passes, scored nine touchdowns, and set a team record for receiving yards in his first season in Washington.

On the Sidelines

Some of the most talented coaches in NFL history led the Redskins into battle during their first 70 seasons. Ray Flaherty coached the team to its first two championships. He was a man of few words, but he always made sure his players were prepared for action.

Coaches came and went often during the team's struggles of the 1950s and 1960s. In 1969, the Redskins hired Vince Lombardi. He coached just one year before he was stricken by cancer, but during that time he gave the team a winning attitude. George Allen followed Lombardi and led a *veteran* team to the **NFC Championship** in 1972.

Washington hired Joe Gibbs in 1981 and started a proud new tradition. Gibbs guided the Redskins to four Super Bowls. No coach was more dedicated to winning. He worked 20-hour days and often slept in his office. Gibbs retired in 1993 and was followed by three top coaches—Norv Turner, Marty Schottenheimer, and Steve Spurrier. He returned to the sidelines in 2004.

Joe Gibbs shows off his three Super Bowl trophies.

One Great Day

No one gave the Redskins much respect during the 1987 season. Though Washington won 11 games, the team looked slow and tired much of the year. Coach Joe Gibbs decided to make a change as the playoffs drew near. He replaced his young quarterback, Jay Schroeder, with 32-year-old Doug Williams. Williams had thrown just one pass for Washington the year before, but he led the team to victory in two exciting playoff games. With Williams in charge, the Redskins found themselves in Super Bowl XXII that January, playing John Elway and the Denver Broncos.

The Broncos were the **favorites** in the big game, and in the first quarter they showed why. Elway played brilliantly, as Denver took a 10–0 lead. The second quarter was a different story.

Williams hit Ricky Sanders for an 80-yard touchdown pass. A few minutes later, Gary Clark caught a pass from Williams for a 27-yard touchdown. The next time Washington had the ball, Timmy Smith ran for a 58-yard score. Williams and Sanders connected again, this time for a 50-yard touchdown. Just before halftime, Williams threw his fourth touchdown of the second quarter, to Clint Didier. In an amazing scoring burst, the Redskins put up 35 points—more than any Super Bowl team had ever scored in a quarter.

In the second half, Washington's offense concentrated on using up as much time as possible. Smith, a last-minute substitute for running back George Rogers, finished with 204 yards to set a Super Bowl record. Led by two players who were expected to do little during the season, the Redskins won their fifth championship by a wide margin. The final score was 42–10.

LEFT: Doug Williams gets ready to launch a long pass in Super Bowl XXII.
ABOVE: Timmy Smith looks for an opening against the Broncos.

Legend Has It

Which Redskin suffered a career-ending injury at the pre-game coin flip?

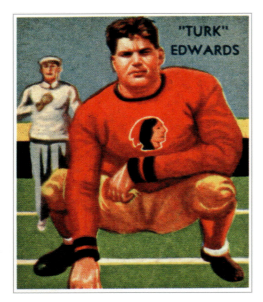

"TURK" EDWARDS

LEGEND HAS IT Turk Edwards did. Edwards was a great blocker and tackler who was later elected to the **Hall of Fame**. As captain of the Redskins, it was his job to call heads or tails when the referee tossed a coin before each game to decide which team would receive the opening kickoff. Moments before a 1940 game against New York, Edwards called the toss, shook hands with his good friend Mel Hein of the Giants, and turned back toward the Washington bench. As he did, his cleats caught in the grass and his knee gave out. Edwards never played again.

ABOVE: Turk Edwards **RIGHT**: Joe Theismann

Who was the NFL's greatest punter?

LEGEND HAS IT that Sammy Baugh was. Baugh's leg was so powerful that he regularly kicked the ball more than 50 yards in the air. He aimed his kicks toward the sidelines, so they could not be returned. Occasionally, Baugh would punt before fourth down. If he saw a chance to pin an opponent back against its own goal line, he would "quick kick" over the heads of the defensive backs. Baugh was the NFL's leading punter four times.

Who was the most superstitious Redskin?

LEGEND HAS IT that Joe Theismann was. Theismann just did not feel right unless he went through a series of pre-game *rituals*. The night before each game, he had to eat a banana split. On game day, he always had pancakes and scrambled eggs for breakfast and then traveled to the stadium with teammates Mark Moseley and Dave Butz. Theismann got to the locker room early enough to read *People* magazine all the way through, but he would not get his ankles taped until everyone else on the team had done so.

It Really Happened

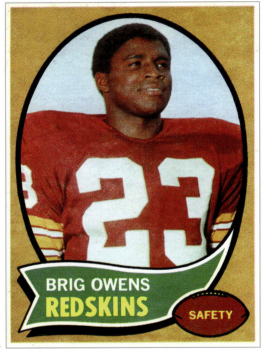

BRIG OWENS
REDSKINS
SAFETY

The Redskins and the New York Giants have been bitter rivals since the 1930s. They have played many unforgettable games, but the wildest surely was their meeting on November 27th, 1966. On that day, the Giants controlled the game everywhere except where it counts—on the scoreboard. New York gained more yards and made more first downs, but the Redskins demolished them by a score of 72–41.

Washington's defense was the difference. They intercepted five passes and kept giving the ball to the offense near the New York goal line, which set up several short touchdown **drives**. Brig Owens, Washington's star defensive back, returned an interception for a touchdown and later ran back a **fumble** for a touchdown. There were so many extra points kicked into the stands during the game that the Redskins were down to their last game ball when time ran out!

Despite all of the touchdowns scored by both teams that day, the game is best remembered for a **field goal**. With time running down and the Redskins way ahead, Charlie Gogolak kicked one through the uprights from 23 yards away for the final three points of the day. That gave Washington the NFL record for most points scored in a regular-season game.

LEFT: Brig Owens **ABOVE**: Charlie Gogolak warms up his leg during a Redskins practice.

31

Team Spirit

Long before the NFL placed clubs in the South, the Redskins were the favorite of football fans from Delaware to Florida. Many continued rooting for Washington even after other teams started playing in the mid-Atlantic region.

Tradition is everything to Redskins fans. They have been cheering for their marching band since 1937 and singing the team's fight song, "Hail to the Redskins," since 1938. In 1962, the Redskins formed an official cheerleading squad. It has been performing for fans ever since—longer than any other group in the NFL.

The loyalty and enthusiasm of Washington fans has made the team one of the most valuable in sports. The Redskins bring in more money each year from tickets, *television rights*, advertising, and souvenirs than any other team in the NFL. The fans are jubilant when the team wins and heartbroken when it loses, but they have always supported their Redskins.

Washington fans have a lot of pride in their team—and in their country.

Timeline

In this timeline, each Super Bowl is listed under the year it was played. Remember that the Super Bowl is held early in the year and is actually part of the previous season. For example, Super Bowl XLI was played on February 4th, 2007, but it was the championship of the 2006 NFL season.

1932
The team plays its first season as the Boston Braves.

1962
Bobby Mitchell leads the NFL with 72 catches.

1937
The Redskins win the NFL Championship in their first season in Washington.

1942
The Redskins defeat the Chicago Bears for their second league title.

1972
Billy Kilmer ties for the NFL lead in touchdown passes.

A souvenir pin from the team's early years.

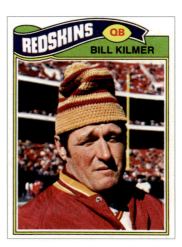

Billy Kilmer

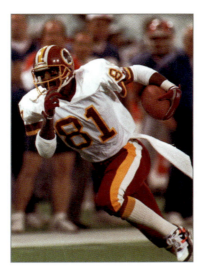

Art
Monk

Stephen
Davis

1984
Art Monk becomes the first player to catch more than 100 passes in a season.

2001
Stephen Davis leads the NFC with 1,432 rushing yards.

1982
Mark Moseley becomes the first kicker to be named NFL MVP.

1988
Doug Williams throws four touchdowns in the second quarter of Super Bowl XXII.

1992
The Redskins defeat the Buffalo Bills in Super Bowl XXVI for their fifth championship.

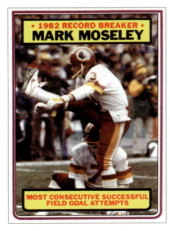

Mark
Moseley

Doug
Williams

35

Fun Facts

SECRETARIES' DAY

On December 7th, 1941, during a Redskins game against the Philadelphia Eagles, an announcement was made for the Secretary of War and Secretary of the Navy to contact the White House immediately. World War II had just started, and they were in the stands rooting for the Redskins!

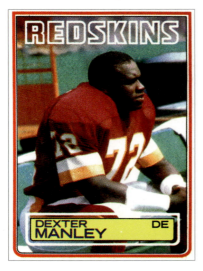

WORD UP

During the 1980s, Washington star Dexter Manley became an inspiration to thousands of children and adults. First he admitted that he could not read, and then he vowed to learn how.

NAME GAME

The 1982 Redskins were a team of nicknames. Their huge offensive line was called the "Hogs." Their tiny pass receivers were called the "Smurfs." The group that danced in the end zone after touchdowns called themselves the "Fun Bunch."

WHAT A DAY!

In 1947, the Redskins proclaimed November 23rd "Sammy Baugh Day." After being honored by the team and its fans, Baugh threw six touchdown passes against the Chicago Cardinals—the league's top team that season!

OLD-TIMERS

Washington coach George Allen liked to trade inexperienced players in their 20s for experienced stars in their 30s. In fact, his Redskins were nicknamed the "Over the Hill Gang." The team owner joked that he had once given Allen two puppies, which he traded for a 10-year-old cat!

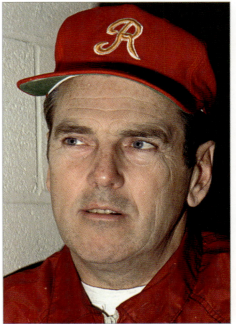

NATIONAL DISASTER

On December 8th, 1940, the Redskins played in the first NFL game broadcast nationally on radio. They met the Chicago Bears for the league championship and lost 73–0!

LEFT: Dexter Manley   **ABOVE**: George Allen

Talking Football

"A winning effort begins with preparation."

—Joe Gibbs, on the importance of practice

"Never try to copy anybody else. Throw a football just like you throw a rock, because it's the natural way of throwing."

—Sonny Jurgensen, on the secret to becoming a good passer

"They were the greatest bunch of fans any player ever had the opportunity to play before."

—Sammy Baugh, on the crowds in Washington's Griffith Stadium

"I could not go to football practice until my homework was done. It taught me priorities."

—Joe Theismann, on the importance of discipline

"The future is now!"

—George Allen, on why he traded future
draft picks for veteran players

"I pioneered for the little guy at the toughest position in football. Name the quarterback, name the receiver. I battled them. Big, little, fast, strong—I battled them all."

—Darrell Green, looking back
on his 20-year career

"What could I do if I couldn't play football? I couldn't do anything—unless I learned how to read and write."

—Dexter Manley, on why he decided to
tell the world he could not read

"In football, you have throwers and you have passers … and then you have Sammy Baugh."

—Hugh Taylor, on his famous
Redskins teammate

LEFT: Joe Gibbs   **RIGHT**: Darrell Green

For the Record

The great Redskins teams and players have left their marks on the record books. These are the "best of the best" …

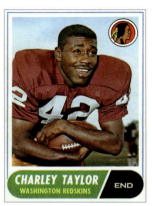

Charley Taylor

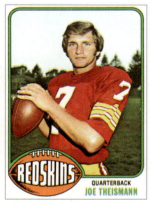

Joe Theismann

REDSKINS AWARD WINNERS

WINNER	AWARD	YEAR
Gene Brito	Pro Bowl co-MVP	1958
Charley Taylor	NFL Rookie of the Year	1964
George Allen	NFL Coach of the Year	1971
Larry Brown	NFL Most Valuable Player	1972
Mike Thomas	NFL Offensive Rookie of the Year	1975
Mark Moseley	NFL Most Valuable Player	1982
Joe Theismann	NFL Offensive Player of the Year	1983
Joe Theismann	NFL Most Valuable Player	1983
John Riggins	Super Bowl XVII MVP	1983
Joe Theismann	Pro Bowl MVP	1984
Doug Williams	Super Bowl XXII MVP	1988
Mark Rypien	Super Bowl XXVI MVP	1992

The "Hogs" congratulate Joe Theismann and John Riggins after a big play.

REDSKINS ACHIEVEMENTS

ACHIEVEMENT	YEAR
NFL Eastern Division Champions	1936
NFL Eastern Division Champions	1937
NFL Champions	1937
NFL Eastern Division Champions	1940
NFL Eastern Division Champions	1942
NFL Champions	1942
NFL Eastern Division Champions	1943
NFL Eastern Division Champions	1945
NFL Eastern Division Champions	1972
NFC Champions	1972
NFC Champions	1982
Super Bowl XVII Champions	1982*
NFL Eastern Division Champions	1983
NFC Champions	1983
NFL Eastern Division Champions	1984
NFL Eastern Division Champions	1987
NFC Champions	1987
Super Bowl XXII Champions	1987
NFL Eastern Division Champions	1991
NFC Champions	1991
Super Bowl XXVI Champions	1991
NFL Eastern Division Champions	1999

*Super Bowls are played early the following year,
  but the game is counted as the championship of this season.*

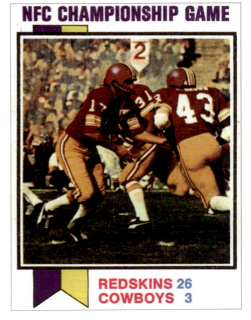

NFC CHAMPIONSHIP GAME

REDSKINS 26
COWBOYS 3

ABOVE: Billy Kilmer hands off to Larry Brown during the 1972 NFC Championship.
BOTTOM RIGHT: Norv Turner, coach of the NFC East champs in 1999.
BOTTOM LEFT: John Riggins in action for the 1983 NFC champs.

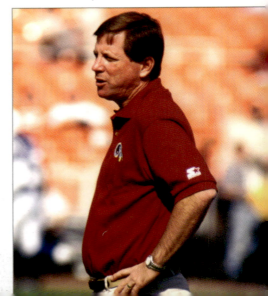

Pinpoints

The history of a football team is made up of many smaller stories. These stories take place all over the map—not just in the city a team calls "home." Match the pushpins on these maps to the Team Facts and you will begin to see the story of the Redskins unfold!

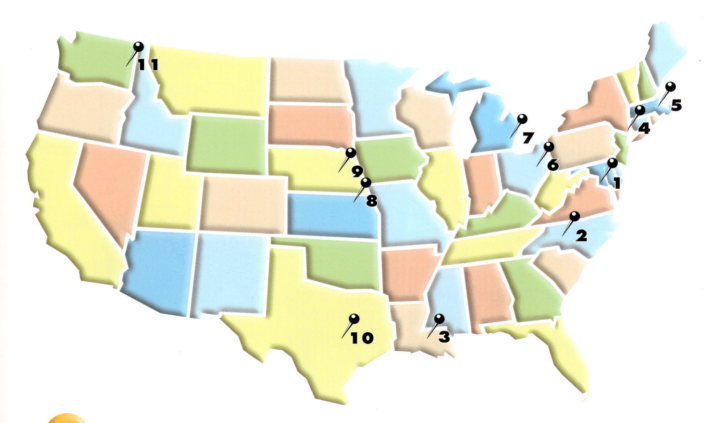

TEAM FACTS

1. Washington, D.C.—*The Redskins have played here since 1937.*
2. Mocksville, North Carolina—*Joe Gibbs was born here.*
3. Zachary, Louisiana—*Doug Williams was born here.*
4. White Plains, New York—*Art Monk was born here.*
5. Boston, Massachusetts—*The team played here from 1932 to 1936.*
6. Akron, Ohio—*Cliff Battles was born here.*
7. Detroit, Michigan—*George Allen was born here.*
8. Seneca, Kansas—*John Riggins was born here.*
9. St. Edward, Nebraska—*Pat Fischer was born here.*
10. Temple, Texas—*Sammy Baugh was born here.*
11. Spokane, Washington—*Ray Flaherty was born here.*
12. Rabahidveg, Hungary—*Charlie Gogolak was born here.*

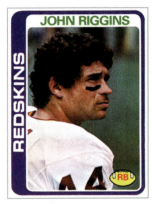

John Riggins

Play Ball

Football is a sport played by two teams on a field that is 100 yards long. The game is divided into four 15-minute quarters. Each team must have 11 players on the field at all times. The group that has the ball is called the offense. The group trying to keep the offense from moving the ball forward is called the defense.

A football game is made up of a series of "plays." Each play starts and ends with a referee's signal. A play begins when the center snaps the ball between his legs to the quarterback. The quarterback then gives the ball to a teammate, throws (or "passes") the ball to a teammate, or runs with the ball himself. The job of the defense is to tackle the player with the ball or stop the quarterback's pass. A play ends when the ball (or player holding the ball) is "down." The offense must move the ball forward at least 10 yards every four downs. If it fails to do so, the other team is given the ball. If the offense has not made 10 yards after three downs—and does not want to risk losing the ball—it can kick (or "punt") the ball to make the other team start from its own end of the field.

At each end of a football field is a goal line, which divides the field from the end zone. A team must run or pass the ball over the goal line to score a touchdown, which counts for six points. After scoring a touchdown, a team can try a short kick for one "extra point," or try again to run or pass across the goal line for two points. Teams can score three points from anywhere on the field by kicking the ball between the goal posts. This is called a field goal.

The defense can score two points if it tackles a player while he is in his own end zone. This is called a safety. The defense can also score points by taking the ball away from the offense and crossing the opposite goal line for a touchdown. The team with the most points after 60 minutes is the winner.

Football may seem like a very hard game to understand, but the more you play and watch football, the more "little things" you are likely to notice. The next time you are at a game, look for these plays:

PLAY LIST

BLITZ—A play where the defense sends extra tacklers after the quarterback. If the quarterback sees a blitz coming, he passes the ball quickly. If he does not, he can end up at the bottom of a very big pile!

DRAW—A play where the offense pretends it will pass the ball, and then gives it to a running back. If the offense can "draw" the defense to the quarterback and his receivers, the running back should have lots of room to run.

FLY PATTERN—A play where a team's fastest receiver is told to "fly" past the defensive backs for a long pass. Many long touchdowns are scored on this play.

SQUIB KICK—A play where the ball is kicked a short distance on purpose. A squib kick is used when the team kicking off does not want the other team's fastest player to catch the ball and run with it.

SWEEP—A play where the ball carrier follows a group of teammates moving sideways to "sweep" the defense out of the way. A good sweep gives the runner a chance to gain a lot of yards before he is tackled or forced out of bounds.

Glossary

BLOCKERS—Players who protect the ball carrier with their bodies.

DRIVES—Series of plays by the offense that "drive" the defense back toward its own goal line.

EAST DIVISION—A group of teams that play in the eastern part of the country. The Redskins play in the NFC East.

FAVORITES—Teams that are expected to win.

FIELD GOAL—A goal from the field, kicked over the crossbar and between the goal posts. A field goal is worth three points.

FUMBLE—A ball that is dropped by the player carrying it.

HALL OF FAME—The museum in Canton, Ohio where football's greatest players are honored. A player voted into the Hall of Fame is sometimes called a "Hall of Famer."

INTERCEPTED—Caught in the air by a defensive player.

LINE OF SCRIMMAGE—The imaginary line that separates the offense and defense before each play begins.

LINEMEN—Players who begin each down crouched at the line of scrimmage.

MOST VALUABLE PLAYER (MVP)—The award given each year to the league's best player; also given to the best player in the Super Bowl and Pro Bowl.

NATIONAL FOOTBALL CONFERENCE (NFC)—One of two groups of teams that make up the National Football League. The winner of the NFC plays the winner of the American Football Conference (AFC) in the Super Bowl.

NATIONAL FOOTBALL LEAGUE (NFL)—The league that started in 1920 and is still operating today.

NFC CHAMPIONSHIP—The game played to determine which NFC team will go to the Super Bowl.

NFC EAST—A division for teams that play in the eastern part of the country.

NFL CHAMPIONSHIP—The game played to decide the winner of the league each year from 1933 to 1969.

NO-HUDDLE OFFENSE—A method of calling plays in which the offense does not get into a huddle. The quarterback tells his teammates what the play is just before he takes the ball from the center.

OVERTIME—The extra period played when a game is tied after 60 minutes.

PLAYOFFS—The games played after the season to determine which teams play in the Super Bowl.

PRO BOWL—The NFL's all-star game, played after the Super Bowl.

PROFESSIONAL—A player or team that plays a sport for money. College players are not paid, so they are considered "amateurs."

ROOKIE—A player in his first season.

SUPER BOWL—The championship of football, played between the winners of the NFC and AFC.

TAILBACK—A position created when football first started. Depending on the play, a tailback would run, throw, or try to catch a pass.

OTHER WORDS TO KNOW

DECADES—Periods of 10 years; also specific periods, such as the 1950s.

DISCIPLINED—Serious and precise.

INSPIRATION—Someone who motivates others with words or deeds.

LAUNDROMATS—Places where the public can use washing machines and dryers.

LOGO—A symbol or design that represents a company or team.

PLEA—An urgent request.

RITUALS—Procedures that are done the same way again and again.

SLUMBER—A long, deep sleep.

TAILBONE—The bone that protects the base of the spine.

TELEVISION RIGHTS—Permission to show a game or program on TV.

TRADITION—A belief or custom that is handed down from generation to generation.

VETERAN—Having many years of experience.

Places to Go

ON THE ROAD

WASHINGTON REDSKINS
1600 FedEx Way
Landover, Maryland 20785
(703) 726-7000

THE PRO FOOTBALL HALL OF FAME
2121 George Halas Drive NW
Canton, Ohio 44708
(330) 456-8207

ON THE WEB

THE NATIONAL FOOTBALL LEAGUE
 • *Learn more about the National Football League*
www.nfl.com

THE WASHINGTON REDSKINS
 • *Learn more about the Washington Redskins*
www.redskins.com

THE PRO FOOTBALL HALL OF FAME
 • *Learn more about football's greatest players*
www.profootballhof.com

ON THE BOOKSHELF

To learn more about the sport of football, look for these books at your library or bookstore:

 • Fleder, Rob–Editor. *The Football Book*. New York, NY: Sports Illustrated Books, 2005.
 • Kennedy, Mike. *Football*. Danbury, CT: Franklin Watts, 2003.
 • Savage, Jeff. *Play by Play Football*. Minneapolis, MN: Lerner Sports, 2004.

Index

PAGE NUMBERS IN **BOLD** REFER TO ILLUSTRATIONS.

The Team

MARK STEWART has written more than 20 books on football, and over 100 sports books for kids. He grew up in New York City during the 1960s rooting for the Giants and Jets, and now takes his two daughters, Mariah and Rachel, to watch them play in their home state of New Jersey. Mark comes from a family of writers. His grandfather was Sunday Editor of *The New York Times* and his mother was Articles Editor of *The Ladies' Home Journal* and *McCall's*. Mark has profiled hundreds of athletes over the last 20 years. He has also written several books about New York and New Jersey. Mark is a graduate of Duke University, with a degree in History. He lives with his daughters and wife Sarah overlooking Sandy Hook, New Jersey.

JASON AIKENS is the Collections Curator at the Pro Football Hall of Fame. He is responsible for the preservation of the Pro Football Hall of Fame's collection of artifacts and memorabilia and obtaining new donations of memorabilia from current players and NFL teams. Jason has a Bachelor of Arts in History from Michigan State University and a Master's in History from Western Michigan University where he concentrated on sports history. Jason has been working for the Pro Football Hall of Fame since 1997; before that he was an intern at the College Football Hall of Fame. Jason's family has roots in California and has been following the St. Louis Rams since their days in Los Angeles, California. He lives with his wife Cynthia and recent addition to the team Angelina in Canton, Ohio.